Develop[illegible] Theologically-rooted Christian Vision in Schools

Paul Rusby
SIAMS QA Inspector, Diocesan and Trust Consultant on Church School Leadership, Spirituality and Christian Distinctiveness in Schools

David Tait
Deputy Director of SIAMS

GROVE BOOKS LIMITED
RIDLEY HALL RD CAMBRIDGE CB3 9HU

Contents

AADE
Anglican Association of Directors of Education

First Impression July 2024
ISSN 2041-0964
ISBN 978 1 78827 403 6

Introduction

1

On the last day of term, one of the Year 4 pupils handed me a card. As I opened it I found myself inexplicably choked with emotion. It said six simple words, simple and yet profound: 'Thank you for helping me grow.'

St Paul writing to the Colossians says, 'Let your roots grow down into him [Jesus], and let your lives be built on him' (Col 2.7). Within the SIAMS inspection framework, the term 'theologically-rooted vision' asks schools to consider 'Who are we?' 'What are we doing here?' and, posed through some inspection questions, 'How then shall we live and learn together?'[1]

This book provides helpful thoughts on this for school leaders, governors, church leaders, trust leaders/trustees, diocesan advisors and all connected with church schools. Whenever we use the term 'leaders' we refer to this whole range of roles. The book does not seek to provide a set of answers, rather some questions prompting reflection on how Christian vision helps adults and pupils to grow and ultimately to flourish. The answer to this, as St Paul reminds us, is found in the life, teachings and example of Jesus—teachings which speak of hope beyond optimism, forgiveness beyond accepting someone is sorry, and love in which all are valued.

2 A Vision-rooted Theology

St John's is a small Church of England primary school of 120 pupils serving a dispersed rural community. The head teacher is new to post and is thinking about the school's Christian vision. She knows that, for the school to be a 'present presence' at the heart of community, it must understand that community well. The head teacher's thinking about the role of church schools has led her to imagine schools not simply as spaces where children come to learn, but as places where community is nurtured and the conditions created that enable people to find fulfilment. She likens this to the difference between a house and a home.

'Growing well' is a term often used in the school community in reference to both the agricultural context and the pupils' growth academically, socially and spiritually. This understanding of place has formed the basis of conversations between the head teacher, governors and local vicar about an appropriate and fruitful Christian vision. The Parable of the Mustard Seed emerged from these conversations as a way in to thinking theologically about the school's context (Matt 13.31–32). An understanding was developed of pupils and adults as seeds, needing the culture of 'water, good soil and sunlight' to grow. As leaders reflected further, they realized that if these elements are replaced with 'curriculum, culture of care for one another and aspiration/ambition' then a Christian vision that speaks powerfully and contextually to this rural community emerges.

The school development partner visited *St Mary's* for the termly visit. At a question posed about challenges, the head teacher paused and responded honestly. He discussed gun crime, food and fuel poverty and a brokenness borne of the unrelenting harshness and fragility of life, as experienced in a community of extreme deprivation. However, as the head teacher stressed to all who wanted to hear the story of St Mary's, this was emphatically only ever the beginning of a journey.

St Mary's, a primary school of 420 pupils, sits physically and practically at the heart of the community. It is a place rooted in the Christian story, and there to serve the common good. The head teacher, with local church and diocesan education team support, had done much thinking about Christian vision. For the Christian faith to have any relevance in this community a number of tenets needed to be given emphasis. That God is not detached but is in this place, and is a God of second (and third and fourth…) chances, was one. Another was that the Christian understanding of God as Father, Son and Holy Spirit illustrates the idea that, although we are all different, nonetheless, we are united in the consistent love and care that we offer—and receive—from God. Thirdly, a belief in resurrection and new life bringing hope, even in the darkest of places, was regarded as pivotal.

Drawing on Isa 40.31, the school's strapline of 'Soaring to the heights together' was all about the need to create a sense of aspiration and togetherness and hope. It was powerful and highly contextually relevant. It spoke theologically of the things of God in this school.

Two Schools, Two Contexts, Two Christian Visions

SIAMS (Statutory Inspection of Anglican and Methodist Schools) explores the interconnected ways in which each school's Christian vision drives its mission and purpose. Each church school is unique. There is no one-size-fits-all approach to inspection. The two schools here are different in a multiplicity of ways. The 2023 SIAMS Framework does not present schools with lists of criteria to meet. Instead, it asks a number of Inspection Questions about impact and it affords leaders the space to explain the school's context and the reasons for decisions and actions. A school's contextually-appropriate, theologically-rooted Christian vision is the driving force for all inspection activity and conversations. The SIAMS Framework highlights and seeks understanding of the theology that underpins a school's Christian vision.

What Does 'Theologically Rooted' Mean?

Theology is the attempt to think and speak about the nature and activity of God in as authentic and consistent a way as human words will allow. The head teachers at St Mary's and at St John's were both speaking of God (so speaking theologically) as they explored their Christian visions.

When Christians speak of God, their ideas are commonly prompted by what is written in the Bible. In the Anglican and Methodist churches, these ideas are often supplemented by Tradition (what the church has taught and practised) and reason (the use of our God-given capacity for rational thought). To this understanding of what constitutes theology, Methodists would also add a fourth element of experience. Together, these four elements form the Methodist Quadrilateral. The theological underpinning of the school's Christian vision must be grounded in Christian beliefs about the nature of God and God's relationship to the world.

In church schools this theological understanding is often linked with a biblical quotation that encapsulates the theological teaching in a memorable way. 'Soaring to the heights' and 'growing well' are two such examples. Others include 'flourishing together' which draws on John 10.10 and 'wonderfully made' which takes inspiration from Ps 139.14.

Church of England and Methodist schools are for everyone. As the Church of England Vision for Education states, they are 'deeply Christian' whilst at the same time 'serving the common good.'[2] Echoing Charles Wesley, they are, 'for all.'[3] Just as a Church of England parish's mission is to all who live there, church schools serve the whole community, not simply those who are professed or committed believers. As John Wesley, from the Methodist tradition, contributed, 'the world is my parish.'[4] As open and inclusive places, it is not expected that all members of the school community will have a common belief about God, or even a belief in God, but leaders must be able to articulate how they respond theologically to their school's context.

How Might a School Go About Establishing a Theologically-rooted Christian Vision?

Some Practical Steps

The Church of England Vision for Education is one example of a theologically-rooted Christian vision.[5] Its language of flourishing is widely understood within church schools, so it is a good starting point for considering what a theologically-rooted Christian vision is and how it might find expression within the unique context of the individual school.

When establishing or developing a Christian vision, leaders may benefit from asking a number of questions. That is where our two head teachers began their journeys. These could include:

What does the original Christian foundation of the school say that the school is for?

- Does it determine that the school should offer a Christian, or an Anglican, or a Methodist education? Is it relevant here and now?

What are the most pressing needs of the community?

- Here, the context in which the school stands is key. There might be a particular need for aspiration or extended horizons; or to learn a generous, accepting, and inclusive attitude towards others; or to create a loving and safe family environment. It is likely that schools will want to do all of this and more, but what are the most pressing community needs? Schools should 'consider the particular circumstances in which they stand.'[6] A simple examination leaders might undertake is to ask: Do I understand the context of my school, and do I know, from this deep understanding, how to respond to it theologically (that is, grounded in Christian beliefs about the nature of God and God's relationship to the world)?

What does the Bible teach about this and about what education in its broadest sense is for?

- Do the teachings and traditions of the church provide any additional wisdom? What does human experience tell us? An exploration of this, making use of the expertise within the local church and other partners should help the school to gain an idea of what the focus of its vision could be.

Having undertaken this initial thinking, leaders might distil their reflections under three interrelated headings: vocation/leadership; theology; and context. Each will act as a conduit for establishing and refining a contextually-appropriate and theologically-rooted Christian vision. Context is fundamental. Leaders are the experts in their school and will determine who to include in discussions and reflections. It will depend on context, capacity and circumstances. There is no right or wrong approach. Leaders are skilled in leading many aspects of work within a community. These conversations fall into this well-understood role and way of working that leaders inhabit on a daily basis.

Questions to Consider

Context

- Who are we as a school/trust? Who do we say we are? Who do others say we are?
- What characterizes the school? What makes us special, unique etc?
- What characterizes the wider community that we serve and/or in which we are located?
- What does the community most need from the school? Which are the most pressing needs? How can we begin to address these? Where do we start?
- How can we best serve the community—in times of joy and fruitfulness and/or in times of challenge and sorrow?

- How can we bring hope and aspiration? How do we speak words of hope where they are needed?
- How can we enable flourishing and fullness of life? What does it look like in our context? What does it look like in our community?

Theology

- What do the Bible, and the teachings and traditions of the church, say about education, in the context of the school? What impact do they have in the here and now?
- What does human experience as a teacher, leader and more generally tell me? How does this link to what I understand by theology?
- The *Church of England Vision for Education, Methodist Schools: Mission, Values and Vision Statement*, diocesan vision or similar have done a lot of this thinking already—what parts of it are most relevant for my school?[7] What has resonance for our community?
- What are we doing here? How can we serve our community?
- What is the 'work of God in this place'? What is it that we are called to do / to be?
- What about the vision we already have? Does it help us to work effectively in our context? Does it need to be refined / reviewed / changed?
- Is it necessary to have a Bible verse as part of the vision? What does it add to the integrity of the vision or to a shared understanding of the vision? What is its purpose?
- How is it possible to keep this theological vision dynamic? How do we listen to the elusive but persistent voice of the Spirit? How can we make the vision provisional (good enough for the current time but growing) rather than set in stone and something no-one dares change?

Vocation

- What drives me? Why do I get up and go to work in my Church of England or Methodist school every morning?
- Why am I called to be a leader? Why here in this school? Why now at this time?
- What is my view of education? What is it for? What is my pedagogical approach?

- Do I have a theology of education? What does the Bible, the church and my understanding of faith tell me matters in education?
- What is my view of leadership? What kind of leader am I/do I aspire to be? What difference does my leadership make?
- Why am I involved in church schools and church school leadership?

If approached in this reflective, focused and structured way, the school's vision will be theologically rooted. Some schools find a Bible verse is useful in terms of having a memorable set of words to hang the vision on. The leaders at St Mary's and St John's adopted different ones. Think about what will work for you. What is important is that the vision has theological roots in accordance with the original purpose of the school; that it shapes and drives the school's work; that it is relevant for the school community; and, crucially, is effective. This does not need to be overcomplicated.

3 A Curriculum Shaped by the Vision

Nestled in the heart of a small rural village, *St Cuthbert's* Church of England Primary School has approximately 40 pupils on roll. Agriculture and rural tourism have been the main source of employment for many years. It was essential to leaders that the rural context was an integral part of the school's vision. 'This reflects the daily experiences of the pupils and many of the staff,' leaders noted.

After much collaboration with members of the local church and school communities, one image of flourishing stood out above all else: the image of growth and good soil. It surrounded the school, physically, with fields of crops and animals for as far as the eye could see. And now, based on the Parable of the Sower from Matthew 13, this image rooted the school theologically: 'Through God's love, we are the good soil so all may grow and flourish at St Cuthbert's.' It spoke to the pupils about the abundance of God's generosity and the beauty of creation which surrounded them. The image of growth was at the very heart of school life. 'How, though,' governors asked, 'does it shape the curriculum?'

A Curriculum Shaped by a Theologically-rooted Vision

This gets to the centre of *Inspection Question 2* about how the curriculum reflects the theologically-rooted vision. Consider, for a moment, your own school curriculum. How might you answer this for yourself?

At its core, any curriculum is developmental from one year group to another. As part of their curriculum review, leaders at St Cuthbert's agreed some non-negotiables. First, their vision must guide their review. The image of growth and good soil should be the lens they looked through. Next, they needed to ensure that elements of the local history, culture and life of the rural area were incorporated into pupils' learning. Finally, they were resolute that the curriculum must provide a window for pupils to look beyond their local area.

Leaders were aspirational for their children. Mindful of the requirements of section 78 of the 2002 Education Act to promote 'the spiritual, moral, social and cultural (SMSC) development of their pupils,' leaders looked at how these elements were covered in their curriculum.[8] They quickly found one of the gaps was that spiritual development did not appear to be an intrinsic part of their curriculum. In addition, although individuals could speak about what spirituality meant to them, there was no shared understanding. Governors reflected on this with some carefully considered questions.

- How does our curriculum provide moments to be still and reflect, to look at the needs of the world, to encounter moments of awe and wonder and, in the words of Rebecca Nye, to be 'open to more?'[9]
- Possibly using a language of spirituality (which is developed in chapter four), how might the curriculum in our school enhance pupils' spiritual development and encourage them to look 'up, in and out?'

Conscious of the lack of diversity in the local area, every opportunity was taken to ensure pupils encountered a wider view of the world. Virtual and physical visits to places of worship were prioritized. The school's set of core texts was updated with much wider reference to diversity. Structural changes were made to the curriculum, so it provided pupils with the good soil in which to grow.

Shaped by the theologically-rooted vision, the curriculum was developed to support pupils to grow in the knowledge of their local area. The intent was also to broaden the horizons of the pupils to help them develop an enhanced knowledge, understanding and ability to evaluate cultures and life beyond their school. Through the lens of their vision, leaders were clear the curriculum must ensure a sense of valuing the worth and dignity of all. Governor monitoring focused on the way the curriculum was shaped by the Christian vision. They asked themselves, 'Does the impact of the curriculum on all pupils, including those who have special educational needs and/or disabilities, and those considered disadvantaged, ensure the school's vision of flourishing is a reality for all?'

Aware of the materialistic world many of the pupils encountered, the word 'value' was vital to leaders in their curriculum review. They reflected on the example of Jesus and the love he showed to all. How, they asked themselves, might our curriculum enhance the way pupils love one another?

Inspection Question 2 offers a useful set of questions in contemplating how the school curriculum reflects the school's vision and, critically, the impact this has on pupils deemed to be disadvantaged. Might a review of these questions enrich the curriculum in your school and help in expressing how it is shaped by your Christian vision and the life and teachings of Jesus?

4 Worship and Spirituality

At a meeting of the governing body of *St Stephen's*, the head teacher shared the outcomes of their recent SIAMS inspection. Although delighted that the inspection recognized how their vision was a lived reality throughout school, governors' thoughts quickly moved to consider how to address the areas for development contained in the report. One particular development area resonated with them: 'Enhance the way that a shared understanding of spirituality exists. This is so adults and pupils can describe the impact of worship on their spiritual development.'

A rather noticeable hush was broken by the head teacher who said how difficult she felt spirituality was to define and how personal it was. Many nodded in agreement. They had recently attended some training from the diocese which offered some suggestions about language which some schools used to demystify the concept of spirituality. Governors were united in wanting to ensure that the theologically-rooted vision might provide the key to unlocking how they could address the inspection area for development. They decided to look again at the Bible verse from Matthew's gospel which their vision was rooted in: 'Let your light shine before others that they may see your good works and glorify your Father in heaven' (Matt 5.16)

'So, how does this help our children and adults express the impact that worship has on them?' one of the governors asked.

Sitting in the heart of a northern coastal town, *St Luke's* vision centred on words they had adapted from John 10.10, 'Life in all its fullness—flourishing together.' The most recent local authority monitoring visit had praised the school for its inclusive culture and the transformative way it met the needs of pupils with special educational needs and/or disabilities (SEND). Their work in ensuring that a similar culture enhanced the learning experiences of some pupils who had recently started the school was similarly praised. This was a school where inclusion was lived out in personalized learning opportunities.

Following some feedback from a pupil voice survey, leaders met to discuss how to make collective worship more inclusive. One of the pupils who encountered difficulties with hearing felt excluded at times and some of the pupils shared how anxious they felt coming into the big hall. A letter from a parent expressed this very clearly. One of the pupils who had recently started the school felt uncomfortable at times with some of the prayers in worship. In response, the worship leader set up a working group to look at how they could ensure worship was more inclusive. They agreed that the starting point for any actions needed to be firmly rooted in the vision. If the theologically-rooted vision truly did drive all actions, as they felt it did, then the answers would be found there.

Dealing with questions about worship, does the theologically-rooted vision provide the answer?

Inspection Question 3 asks the school to consider: 'How is collective worship enabling pupils and adults to flourish spiritually?' This question brings together the concepts of worship, flourishing and spirituality; the dynamic process of exploration of how they relate to each other in practice is called theology. Many Christians believe that all people, everywhere, are created out of an overspilling of God's love, and all have a need to return that love in worship. Worship is both individual and social. Collective worship in a church school presupposes that all have a need to worship, whilst recognizing that it is an affront to how we are uniquely made to attempt to compel anyone to worship, so the approach by worship leaders should always be invitational, and never presuppose personal Christian commitment.

Whether as a class, or as a whole school, collective worship is a time to come together. Within the busyness of the day many adults and pupils speak of worship as a precious time which binds the school community together. In times of increasing pressure on school timetables, this time can often be an oasis, a special moment of quiet, providing time for spiritual flourishing. How might staff in your school describe this time? Would they feel that worship is a time for spiritual refreshment? In making this time, schools mirror the way Jesus took time out of the busyness of each day just to be still and to pray.

Questions to Consider

- Why is it that you gather to worship? Yes, there is the legal requirement and SIAMS inspections, but if these did not exist, what is it that makes gathering together for collective worship a special part of the day for the adults and pupils in your school?

- How does the theologically-rooted Christian vision shape worship so it is an essential aspect of each day and nourishes pupils and adults spiritually?
- How does the theologically-rooted vision shape a shared understanding of spirituality?

As governors at St Stephen's noted, the concept of spirituality can be challenging to articulate, sometimes creating a barrier in enabling people to express the impact of worship on them. Spirituality is relational. At the heart of spirituality is a sense of encounter and connectedness with other people, ourselves and the possibility of something / someone beyond us.[10] This refers to what Christians might speak of as God.

Maybe take a moment to ponder, what do you understand by spirituality and when did you last feel spiritually nourished and refreshed? For some it might be the feeling when standing watching the sunrise in the morning, for others it might be the goosebumps moment when a lone chorister sings the first verse of *Once in Royal David's City* at the start of a carol service. The team at St Stephen's found that asking the question about where we feel spiritually nourished brought a wide variety of answers, highlighting the uniqueness of each person. For many schools this is an accessible, and often profound, conversation to share. Might it be useful in your school?

Moving from that conversation to establishing a language which pupils and adults can own is an essential step in enabling all to describe how worship enhances their spirituality. Debbie Helme and Joanne Wetherall, for instance, use the language of 'Wows' (awe and wonder moments), 'Ows' (moments of hurt) and 'Nows' (stillness and reflection) to create a lexicon accessible to all ages.[11] Working with schools, I have found the language of 'In' (looking at how the experience impacts on me personally), 'Out' (how the experience encourages me to look out to others) and 'Up' (how the experience connects me to God) to be useful language for adults and pupils to describe spiritual moments.[12] Simple in structure, the responses which often come from this accessible language can be profound.

So how might this help the governors at St Stephen's in connecting their theologically-rooted vision to a shared understanding of spirituality?

Again, the key is to go back to the biblical text from Matt 5.16 in which the vision is rooted. The head teacher invited governors to be part of worship and see how the vision and the language of 'in, out and up' might help adults and pupils to express the impact of worship on them.

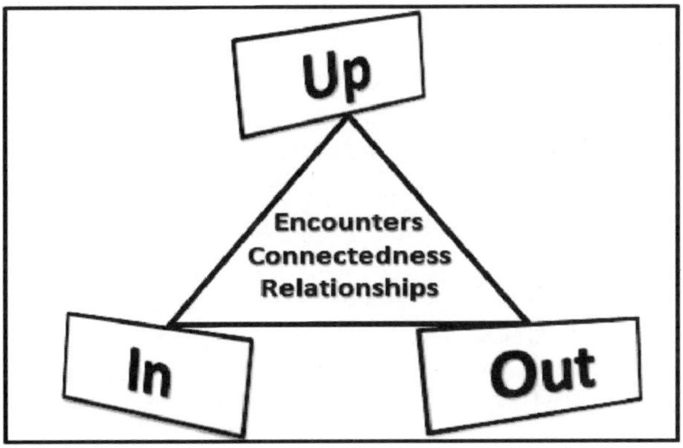

'In'—a word to encourage people in looking inwards, reflecting, noticing how they are feeling

- When governors fed back they noted that the word 'in' helped pupils to describe the impact of moments of stillness and reflections about themselves. They linked this to the word 'your,' as in 'let your light shine.' Looking inwards, governors described a personal sense of inner peace and calm which they encountered during worship. The simple word 'in' provided a language to help describe this.

'Out'—a word to encourage people to look to the needs of others, to be a good neighbour

- During collective worship, the head teacher asked the pupils to reflect on the impact of the actions of the good Samaritan and how this might encourage to look towards the needs of others. One of the foundation governors was deeply moved by this. She highlighted how the word 'out' enabled her to express how the worship ignited in her a sense of seeking to help those she encountered who might be in need. She linked this to the word 'others' within the vision.

'Up'—a word to encourage people to look beyond, to a sense of the divine, the transcendent, to God

- Whilst listening to the youngest pupils singing the hymn, *He's Got the Whole World in His Hands,* another governor spoke of a sense of connectedness to God, which the pupil described using the term 'up'; the song metaphorically guided his eyes upwards.[13] Governors linked this to the final words of their vision which speaks of giving glory to 'your Father in heaven.'

Through the use of the words 'in,' 'out' and 'up,' governors felt they could express a range of different ways in which worship enabled them to flourish spiritually. The Annual SIAMS Report for 2023 notes that:

> in schools where spirituality is understood, there is a shared language for both adults and pupils to express and discuss spiritual matters, including their own spiritual development.[14]

Many schools might find themselves in a similar position to the governors of St Stephen's in seeking to explore how their vision shapes their understanding of spirituality and the way this understanding is readily, and naturally, expressed by pupils and adults.

Questions to Consider

- Can you think of a moment where you, as an adult, felt spiritually nourished at school?
- Is spirituality seen as just part of the curriculum and worship or is it a golden thread that permeates through the very culture of what it means to be a church school?
- Does being a worship leader enhance a child's own spirituality? For some pupils might leading worship actually be a barrier to their own spiritual development?
- How does the range of activities within worship (such as use of music, images, silence, drama, video, Bible reading, prayer, reflection time) enhance the spiritual development of everyone?

The Way the Vision Shapes How Collective Worship is Inclusive, Inspirational and Invitational

Staff at St Luke's felt very confident at expressing how their worship was inspirational. Having pupils and adults with a range of faiths and views, they had looked carefully at the use of inclusive language. Prayers now were also much more invitational in style. Pupils and adults were invited to say 'Amen' if they wanted to make the prayer their own. The language of 'We believe' changed to 'Christians believe' and then changed again to 'Some Christians believe,' highlighting similarities and differences in belief and tradition. Pupil voice monitoring highlighted a sense that worship was invitational to all.

Questions to Consider

- When was the last time your school evaluated how worship in your school is invitational, inclusive and inspirational? Who was asked? What was asked? What changed as a result of the monitoring? For instance:
- How inclusive is worship to adults and pupils holding a range of faiths and views? How is this shaped by the school's theologically-rooted vision?
- How is invitational language shared with visiting worship leaders to ensure consistency?
- How do visiting worship leaders (such as an 'Open the Book' group from the local church) enhance the way worship is considered to be inspirational?
- How does worship impact on relationships and behaviour throughout the school. Does it inspire a culture of forgiveness when mistakes are made? How is this inspired by the life and teachings of Jesus?
- How is class-based worship monitored? How are staff supported so it is as equally invitational and inspirational as whole school worship?

As well as being invitational and inspirational, leaders at St Luke's felt that worship was inclusive, too. However, a letter from a parent whose child has SEND caused them to stop and reflect on whether worship at St Luke's really did create an environment where worship was accessible to all. The pupil in question found time in the large hall overwhelming. After discussions, changes came about which ensured that the vision of fullness of life for all became a living reality for the pupil who had felt excluded from worship. A safe place was established in the hall next to a trusted adult. Ear defenders were purchased and a safe exit strategy was agreed for times the pupil felt overwhelmed. This made leaders wonder if other pupils or adults felt excluded, so a working party was established. To ensure one pupil who had additional hearing needs felt included, leaders decided that all pupils would learn British Sign Language to use for songs and prayers. This made a difference by including that one pupil but also enhanced worship for all. It led staff to ponder: 'Does our vision about "fullness of life" enable all to flourish and not just some?'

Questions to Consider

Maybe some of the questions the working group at St Luke's asked themselves might be useful questions to ask about your school:

- Is personalized support in worship included in Education Health Action Plans (EHCPs) and for pupils who have SEND?
- Are there pupils who have suffered trauma, for whom symbols, such as candles, might be distressing?
- Are practical items such as ear defenders or walking in next to a trusted adult in place for pupils who need such support?
- Do the images used of biblical figures highlight Christianity as a global faith?
- How are diversity and difference celebrated in worship? What might it feel to be different whilst sitting in worship in this school?
- Whilst being distinctively Christian and theologically rooted, how does this vision reflect the different views and faiths within the school? How does this affect the provision of worship?
- The Church of England's own Vision for Education is predicated on a vision for the 'common good of the whole community.'[15] Is this a living reality in your school? How is this shaping worship?

For the theologically-rooted vision to shape worship, it must be organic, central to the beating heart of daily school life. It must, each day, emerge incarnationally from the aspirational and messy context of the school. It is about taking seriously an ever-changing context as governors, staff, families, the local church and pupils reflect together on what their context means, as a church school, in the light of what is learned from Scripture, the life of Jesus and the teachings of the church. The way the theologically-rooted vision shapes worship is therefore practical and useful in moving forward the daily worshipping life of the school. For the vision to be effective in shaping worship, rather than merely abstract, it needs to be about people and relationships more than it is about theological principles and rule-bound concepts.

Questions to Consider

- How do you feel the theologically-rooted vision in your school shapes worship and ensures that worship is invitational, inclusive and inspirational?
- How does it enable pupils and adults to flourish spiritually? Is there a shared language and understanding within school of how to express this?

A Culture in Which All Are Treated Well

5

How does your school's theologically-rooted christian vision create a culture in which pupils and adults are treated well?

> 'Dear Mrs Jones,' the letter began, 'It has taken me some time to write this letter—but I know I have to. I'm embarrassed that I need to explain our circumstances and request some assistance with the Lake District trip costs, if you possibly can. This trip is important to my children but we just can't afford it. I'm so sorry…' As she read the letter, Mrs Jones, the head teacher, felt the pain of the parent asking for some help with the financial cost of the residential trip to the Lake District later that year. A week later, at the spring term governors' meeting of *St Chad's* C of E Primary School, item 5 was a review of the school's charging policy. The recent correspondence from the parent was confidentially mentioned. Mr Richards, one of the foundation governors, suggested that, before their discussion, they remind themselves again of the school's vision, theologically rooted in St Paul's First Letter to the Thessalonians (1 Thess 5.11). He read out the words of their vision: 'Encourage one another and build each other up.' 'If residential experiences are important, how is our vision a living reality for all our families, including those who are disadvantaged?' Mr Richards asked and then continued, 'How does our vision practically ensure an equitable culture within our school?'

St Paul's injunction to 'Encourage one another and build each other up' is as applicable today as when first written (1 Thess 5.11). If decisions by leaders directly flow from a desire to 'encourage and build up,' how, then, does the theological rootedness of this vision directly affect the culture within the school? Governors at St Chad's updated their charging policy to enhance equity of provision in their school so that all pupils now have access to residential trips. Pragmatically, they understood that budgets are finite and were minded of their responsibility to balance their budget. However, Paul's instruction, central to life at the school, spurred them on to look again at their own spending decisions. This included contacting their local church to request financial assistance with establishing a discretionary fund to support the needs of families.

The governors wanted pupils to encounter practically the school's theological vision as a transformative living reality. With further reflection, they asked themselves, 'Why did she have to write at all, and who else in our school community is in need but we don't know about it?' At the heart of church schools is the example of Jesus. His teachings are countercultural against a dominant culture where you only matter if you are cost-effective and successful (defined by many as 'rich in resources'). As the governors at St Chad's did, you might feel it useful to review how the vision in your school creates a culture in which pupils and adults are treated well. This could include considering how your charging policy ensures equity of provision for all, including those considered vulnerable and/or disadvantaged.

Maybe it is also useful to consider how the culture created in your school influences areas such as staff development, adult and pupil well-being, good mental health and resilience. If the culture is explicitly rooted in the practice of building each other up and developing resilience, might that support schools with the retention and recruitment of staff? One helpful source of information on this is the Church of England Education Office document on flourishing in schools. In the introduction, Paul Butler writes about 'institutions that themselves work together in a vibrant ecology focused on the flourishing of all.'[16] Does such an image of vibrancy and positivity describe the school you are connected with? If so, how might this be directly guided by the school's theologically-rooted Christian vision?

Questions to Consider

- Does your school have a vibrant ecology which is focused on the flourishing of all and rooted in the example and teachings of Jesus?
- How does this impact on policies such as appraisal, charging and staff development?
- Schools have nominated adults with responsibility for First Aid and Mental Health First Aid which support physical and emotional well-being. Who is the 'go-to' person in your school for spiritual well-being? If we think about our wholeness of being, who helps with 'spiritual first aid'?
- At St Chad's school, Mr Richards asked his fellow governors: 'How does our vision practically ensure an equitable culture within our school?' Consider how those in your school might answer this?
- How are the words of the vision a living reality for all adults and pupils within the school, such as those which root the vision at St Giles' C of E Primary in the example below?

'Not the story of the good Samaritan again,' one Year 6 pupil whispered to his friend, Sam, as they sat, cross legged, on the wooden floor of the main hall at St Giles' C of E Primary School during worship. The school's vision of 'Love God, love your neighbour and love yourself,' rooted in the parable from Luke's gospel meant that the pupils were very familiar, maybe too familiar, with the actions of the priest, Levite and the good Samaritan (Luke 10. 25–42).

As the story came to an end, the head teacher announced he had the five most important words in the story. Intrigued, Sam sat up to listen. Quoting from Luke 10.37, the head teacher lifted his left hand, with each digit raised to represent a word. As he spoke, 'Go…and…do… the…same' he challenged all in the hushed hall to put these five words into action.

Three hours later, pupils were playing outside at lunchtime. As he ran out to play the regular lunchtime game of football, Sam noticed one of the Year 4 boys looking rather upset. The boy explained how he had no one to play with. In an instant, Sam invited him to join in with their game. An invitation, so simple, and yet, in that moment, completely transformative for the young child who experienced Jesus' words, 'Go and do the same,' lived out in the actions of Sam.

At St Giles' there is a connectedness between the culture of care that is explicitly inspired by the teachings of Jesus and the positive impact this has on others. It is relational. Consequently, the culture has a positive impact on the experiences pupils have in school, through the way the vision is actively lived out. Jesus' words, 'Go and do the same,' guide the actions of pupils and adults in the school.

One pupil, who came into school upset because her grandmother was poorly, was met at the door by two of her friends. Instinctively, they could tell something was wrong and they wanted to help. That simple act of kindness set her up for the rest of the day, enabling her to achieve. Asked why they had been so attentive, her friends shrugged their shoulders and simply said they were just trying to 'do the same.'

Jesus' words were so deeply embedded in the school that they were lived out in a natural and unenforced way. The friends' behaviour demonstrated how the school's vision was embedded in the everyday language of love—love embodied through the teachings, life, death and resurrection of Jesus. Consider, how naturally lived out is the culture in your school? Does it lead to all being treated well? Is it a culture fundamental to all human thriving? How might this be seen in areas such as anti-bullying, prejudice and issues which lead to good mental health?

This takes us back to the core of the all the inspection questions which seek to answer, 'How then shall we live and learn together?'[17] In our context as a church school, surely, if Jesus' words of love are at the heart of our answer, then our theologically-rooted vision is more than a set of words. It is the very culture which naturally enables all to flourish. A culture where hope (rather than just a sense of optimism) comes directly through the school's vision. Or, in those challenging moments, where might forgiveness be encountered beyond a simple 'Sorry'? Love, hope, forgiveness are values that can apply to any school. Within a church school, these are rooted in the life, ministry, death and resurrection of Jesus. They are central to a Christian culture where all are treated well. Do you sense this is a reality in your school?

In his book, *Incarnational Mission*, Sam Wells says that he believes '*with*' is the most important word in the Christian faith.[18] It speaks of incarnation, the Christian belief in God sending Jesus as Emmanuel, God with us, as a sign of his love for all people (Matt 1.23). It resonates with a sense of walking alongside each other, as embodied in the parable where Jesus introduces the figure of the Good Samaritan and where he walks alongside his disciples on the road to Emmaus (Luke 24. 13–25). St Giles' school vision is theologically rooted in the words of Jesus within the Parable of the Good Samaritan. In this school, 'being with' others is lived out in their culture of treating others well. The power of 'being with' is felt by adults and pupils in their emotions of joy, pain, success, grief and brokenness. They feel known, loved and cared for. Through this, the culture actively lives out Jesus' teachings and actions.

Questions to Consider

- Is the theologically-rooted vision in your school so embedded and understood that it is the natural language of all, creating a culture where all feel known and loved?
- How does the culture enable adults and pupils to encounter hope, beyond optimism, at times where they might feel a sense of failure?
- Thinking of power dynamics in schools, does the culture create openness where staff can be vulnerable in admitting to struggling without worry of possible repercussions?
- How does the culture in your school ensure all, including those deemed to be vulnerable and/or disadvantaged are helped at difficult times?

An Active Culture of Justice and Responsibility

6

Inspection Question 5: How does the school's theologically-rooted Christian vision create an active culture of justice and responsibility?

'Working Together, Valuing All, Learning for Life'

These are the bold claims set out in the vision at *St Michael's,* a two-form entry junior school serving an area of relative deprivation and geographical isolation at the edge of a small coastal town. St Michael's folk, however, do not talk much about their 'vision' and certainly not their 'theologically-rooted Christian vision.' You will not find detailed information about it on their website.

This is intentional. The head teacher is clear that whilst their work is rooted in the Christian story and is faithful to their status as a church school, they have intentionally not expressed their vision in overtly theological language. This is because to do so would present a barrier to many of the community, where literacy levels are low and many do not have a positive personal experience of schools or formal institutions. To present the vision in formal theological language would render aspects of the school inaccessible to those it loves and serves. It would, therefore, be in tension with the intended purpose of enabling the flourishing of all God's children and being a place of welcome for all, irrespective of their own background or beliefs.

Instead, the school speaks of its 'strapline.' That is how they articulate vision here. In conversations with leaders, reference is often made to the school being a place that 'seeks justice,' as this is often the most pressing need in the community. It is a school that looks outward to serve, as well as inward to nurture and heal. This justice seeking is expressed in, and woven through, the school's strapline:

Working Together

The gospels are full of accounts of Jesus' intimate encounters with those of each and every background—the wise and the powerful, the humble and the lowly. Each and every one is called, by invitation and without compulsion, into a relationship with Jesus who has come to give life, break down barriers and establish justice. In their community they draw on the account of the feeding of the 5000 to demonstrate their belief that, by working together, the unique, inimitable worth of every individual is brought, through the work of the school, to fruition (Matt 14.13–21). It is this flourishing of each person through working together in community, as God intends, that motivates and inspires them.

Valuing All

The gospels, the teaching of the church and the Christian story demonstrate that God values all, unequivocally. In their community they draw on the account of the lost sheep to demonstrate their belief in infectious, generous, ceaseless and overflowing love (Luke 15.1–7). By valuing all, as God intends that they should, they demonstrate that true community is found where there are no outsiders and all are known and loved. They go the extra mile in order to be attentive to the needs of all in their community. Their differences are their strengths.

Learning for Life

Jesus was a great storyteller and teacher. In their community they draw on the account of Jesus aged twelve in the Temple to demonstrate their belief in the value of lifelong learning and they cherish the model of Jesus as teacher (Luke 2.41–52). Through a rich and engaging curriculum which reflects their Christian vision, establishes opportunities to seek justice and is rooted in their local context, they ensure that they are a learning community committed to the academic flourishing of their pupils.

'This is our strapline,' the school will tell anyone who cares to visit. It is a brief summary of who they are and why they do what they do. It encapsulates their Christian vision in three simple steps:

- Working Together: We Feed
- Valuing All: We Find
- Learning for Life: We Flourish

It is clear that there is a deep and palpable understanding of the context in which St Michael's operates, demonstrating its rootedness in the community it serves. Leaders understand their community and its needs, so are well placed to serve. The appending of a Bible verse to the general articulation of this vision in the strapline would be a barrier and has been avoided. Similarly, theological language, understood in an academic sense, has also been jettisoned. The school is considered and deliberate in all it does. It seeks to create opportunities to connect with its community, rather than barriers to understanding or participation. The work that the school undertakes in terms of advocacy, encouraging its pupils to make ethical choices and take responsibility, alongside establishing partnerships, all flows seamlessly from this rooting in the Christian story.

Looking Outward

Inspection Question 4 focuses primarily on the internal culture of a school. *Inspection Question 5* then builds on this, looking outwards, towards others. This question is challenging schools as to how they are communities where people look beyond self.

Jesus created such an active culture of justice and responsibility, often using terms such as 'go' and 'do' as he challenged his disciples to transform lives through their own actions. The Torah, which would have been at the heart of Jesus' family and social life, is sharply focused on revealing God's justice and the responsibility that each should take for the other, such as widows, orphans and strangers. Jesus imbibed this culture from childhood. The words of Micah speak of this: 'Do justice, love kindness, and walk humbly with your God' (Micah 6.8), as does the prophet Amos, who declared, 'Let justice roll on like a river, righteousness like a never-failing stream!' (Amos 5.24). Jesus questioned the *status quo* when the religious and social culture were in conflict with basic human need. Indeed, this resonates with Jesus' own direction in Matt 22.39 to 'Love your neighbour.' For many schools, it is these and similar exhortations in Scripture that provide a language which motivates and inspires social action and courageous advocacy as they focus on being outward looking, seeking to support those in their community and beyond where they feel there is a sense of injustice.[19]

Other schools look to inspirational examples from Christian history to support their thinking around justice. Oscar Romero is one such example. His story is a poignant twentieth-century example of a church leader who pursued his vision of God's justice—and was martyred for it. Of course, only very rarely does the cost of such social action have to be martyrdom, but there is always a cost. The words of Archbishop Romero, 'Aspire not to have more, but to be more,' have provided a template for this sense of social action to be infused throughout the curriculum in some schools.[20] They are words which go to the heart of human flourishing and are words which might seem countercultural within what is often seen as a materialistic society. However, that sense of being countercultural is at the heart of Jesus' message to 'love your neighbour.'

A similarly inspirational individual from the twentieth century is Dr Martin Luther King. King challenged his followers with these words, 'Life's most persistent and urgent question is, 'What are you doing for others?''[21] He lived out a challenge to be outward looking, intrinsically underpinned by Jesus' words of love and practical kindness towards all those he encountered. His quest for justice can be helpful for schools in understanding their need to seek justice.

From the Methodist tradition, Susanna Wesley, known as the 'mother of Methodism,' is another such inspirational individual. Although she is most widely known as the mother of John and Charles Wesley, the founders of Methodism, she was also a theologian, writer and teacher in her own right.[22] Her example has great resonance for Methodist and joint Methodist-Anglican schools as they consider issues pertaining to justice and responsibility. Similarly, the life of Queen Elizabeth II is one that provides inspiration for many. Her role as a servant queen whose life was lived through the prism of servant leadership with a heart for justice demonstrates how power can be worn lightly, creating a culture of justice and responsibility towards others.[23]

At the point where the theologically-rooted vision emphatically leads to justice seeking, it becomes one of the 'whys' of the school. William Booth, the founder of the Salvation Army, was reported as unable to attend a conference at which he was due to speak. In the days before text messages and social media, he sent a telegram to the conference organizers with his apologies which just had one word, 'Others.'[24] In that one word, he inspired those attending to be outward looking, putting love into action. Might a school be bold enough to have such a one word vision? A word which is so embedded in Christ's message of love for others, that its everyday language, its reason to be, would have at its heart that active culture of justice, responsibility and courageous advocacy?

Questions to Consider

- What is meant by courageous advocacy? How is it a reflection of the school's theologically-rooted Christian vision? What does it look like in practice?
- What evidence is there that pupils are empowered to act for justice and are encouraged/enabled to make ethical choices?
- If the school has partnerships (in the UK or elsewhere in the world), why do they have them? How are they an expression of the school's vision? What do leaders intend to achieve through them? How do they know if they are meaningful?

7

Conclusion

Gardeners know only too well that, without roots, fruit will not appear. The SIAMS Framework is unapologetically bold in using the language of growth. Through a vision rooted in the Christian story, it speaks of flourishing: an image of abundance highlighted in Jesus' acclamation of coming that all 'may have life and have it abundantly' (John 10.10). This book prompts us to look back at the inspection questions, one by one, through the lens of growth and abundance. It encourages us to ask, 'Where are there opportunities for abundance in the curriculum, in worship and spirituality, in the culture of the school, in opportunities to create a culture of justice and in the effectiveness of religious education?'

It encourages governors, church leaders, school leaders, trust leaders, PCC members and all involved in church schools to reflect on their own school and ask questions which get to the heart of its Anglican or Methodist foundation:

- Is our theologically-rooted vision relevant to those we serve?
- How does it enable all to flourish?
- Are Jesus's words of 'life in all its fullness' a living reality for all in our church school?

How would you feel if the Christian vision inspired a member of staff, a parent or a pupil to write a card that said, *'Thank you for helping me grow'*?

Notes

1 The Statutory Inspection of Anglican and Methodist Schools, *SIAMS Framework 2023 (2022)*, available at https://www.churchofengland.org/sites/default/files/2022-11/siams-framework-september-2023.pdf

2 Church of England Education Office, *Church of England Vision for Education: Deeply Christian, Serving the Common Good* (London: Archbishops' Council, 2016).

3 C Wesley, from the hymn *Let earth and heaven agree* (358 in the current Methodist Hymn Book). The final verse ends: 'For all my Lord was crucified, for all, for all my saviour died.'

4 J Wesley, *Journal* (June 1739).

5 Church of England Education Office, *op cit.*

6 J Wesley, *Advice to the People Called Methodist* (October 1745).

7 Methodist Church, *Methodist Schools Mission, Values and Vision Statement* available at: missionvaluesvision-statement-final-feb-2022-on-website.pdf (methodistschools.org.uk).

8 Department for Education (DfE), *Promoting Fundamental British Values as Part of SMSC in Schools Departmental Advice for Maintained Schools* (Crown Copyright, 2014).

9 R Nye, *Children's Spirituality* (London: Church House Publishing, 2009).

10 A Casson, 'Paying Attention to the Spiritual Flourishing of Young Children in Church Toddler Groups: A Scoping Study Evaluating the Feasibility of a Research Study' in *This Context* https://www.mdpi.com/2077-1444/14/2/236 (accessed March 2024).

11 D Helme and J Wetherall, *The Language of Spirituality in Collective Worship* (Gloucester: Jumping Fish Ltd, 2020).

12 P Rusby, *Spirituality and Flourishing* (Durham: Newcastle and Durham Diocese Joint Education Team Conference, 2023).

13 *Mission Praise,* No 225 (London: HarperCollins Publishers, 1999).

14 *The Annual Report of the National Director of the Statutory Inspection of Anglican and Methodist Schools 2022–2023:* https://www.churchofengland.org/sites/default/files/2023-09/siams-annual-report-2022-2023.pdf

15 Church of England Education Office, *Church of England Vision for Education, op cit.*

16 Church of England Education Office, *Church of England Vision for Education: Our Hope for a Flourishing Schools System: Deeply Christian, Serving the Common Good* (London: Archbishops' Council, 2023).

17 The National Society, *The Statutory Inspection of Anglican and Methodist Schools Framework* (2022), p 8.

18 S Wells, *Incarnational Mission: Being with the World* (Norwich: Canterbury Press, 2018) p 9.

19 Courageous advocacy is a well-understood concept in church schools. See: C Weir and D Holloway, *Courageous Advocacy* (Christian Aid and Church of England Education Office, 2021); R Hopkins, *Courageous Advocacy and Political Neutrality in Schools* (Grove Education booklet eD57).

20 Vatican News, *Remembering Oscar Romero (2020)*, available at: https://www.vaticannews.va/en/church/news/2020-03/oscar-romero-forty-years-assassination-anniversary0.html (accessed December 2023).

21 M L King Jr, *Strength to Love Sermon: Three Dimensions of a Complete Life* (New York: Harper and Row, 1963) p 72.

22 350th Anniversary of Susanna Wesley's Birth, available at: 350th Anniversary of Susanna Wesley's Birth (methodist.org.uk) (accessed January 2024).

23 C Butcher and M Greene, *The Servant Queen and the King she Serves* (London: Bible Society, 2016).

24 The Salvation Army Ridge Meadows Ministries, available at: https://ridgemeadowssa.ca/others/ (accessed December 2023).